Word Bird's

Halloween Words

Published in the United States of America by The Child's World®, Inc.
PO Box 326
Chanhassen, MN 55317-0326
800-599-READ
www.childsworld.com

Project Manager Mary Berendes
Editor Katherine Stevenson, Ph.D.
Designer Ian Butterworth

Library of Congress Cataloging-in-Publication Data
Moncure, Jane Belk.
Word Bird's Halloween words / by Jane Belk Moncure.
p. cm.
ISBN 1-56766-627-2 (alk. paper)
1. Vocabulary—Juvenile literature. 2. Halloween—Juvenile literature.
[1. Vocabulary. 2. Halloween. 3. Holidays.]   I. Title: Halloween words. II. Title.
PE1449 .M529 2001
428.1—dc21
00-011097

Word  Bird's™

Halloween Words

by Jane Belk Moncure

illustrated by Chris McEwan

Word Bird made a...

word house.

"I will put Halloween
words in my house,"
said Word Bird.

Word Bird put in these words:

Who-o-o-o-o will you see on Halloween night?

Halloween

OCTOBER

1	2	3	4	5	6	7
8	9	10	11	12	13	14
15	16	17	18	19	20	21
22	23	24	25	26	27	28
29	30	31				

October 31

pumpkin patch

jack-o'-lantern

Halloween colors

black cats

scarecrow

witches

brooms

bats

haunted house

ghosts

"Boo!"

owls

"Who-oo-o."

masks

monsters

costumes

parade

Halloween party

safety bug

"Trick or treat."

Can you read these Halloween

Halloween

scarecrow

October 31

witches

pumpkin patch

brooms

jack-o'-lantern

bats

Halloween colors

haunted house

black cats

words with Word Bird?

ghosts

monsters

"Boo!"

costumes

owls

parade

Halloween party

"Who-oo-o."

safety bug

masks

"Trick or treat."

You can make a Halloween word house. You can put Word Bird's words in your house and read them, too.

Can you think of other Halloween words to put in your word house?